Dinosaur Jokes

Einstein Sisters

KidsWorld

The word **dinosaur** means
"terrible lizard."

Dino Facts

The biggest
dinosaurs ate plants.
The fastest dinosaurs
were meat eaters.

A
paleontologist
is a scientist who
studies
dinosaurs.

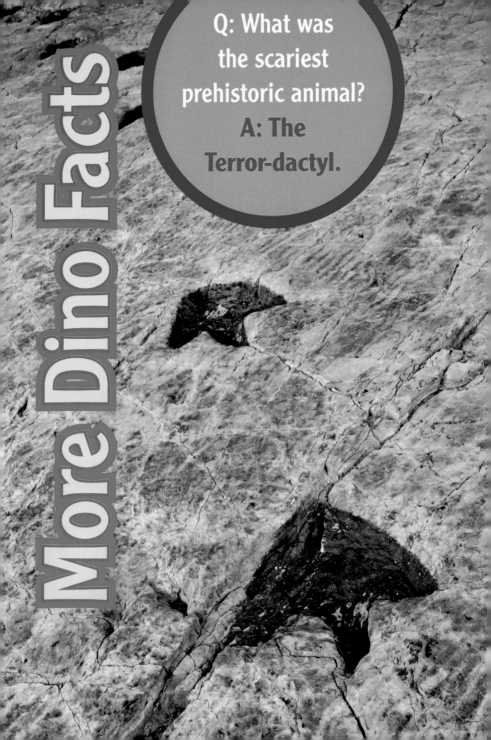

More Dino Facts

Q: What was the scariest prehistoric animal?
A: The Terror-dactyl.

Sometimes a fossil has an imprint of the dinosaur's skin. Paleontologists can tell if the skin was rough or smooth. They can even tell if the dinosaur had feathers.

Paleontologists often don't find a complete skeleton. They have to guess how some parts of the dinosaur looked.

The spikes on its tail were almost 1 metre long. Stegosaurus used its tail to defend itself.

Stegosaurus

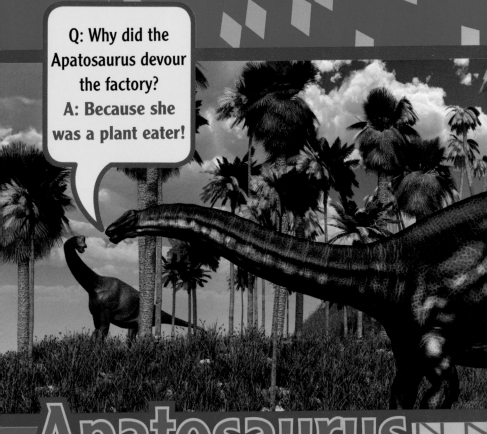

Q: Why did the Apatosaurus devour the factory?
A: Because she was a plant eater!

Apatosaurus

Apatosaurus was one of the **largest animals** to ever live on Earth. It was **27 metres** long. That's almost as long as a full-sized basketball court. It only ate plants.

Apatosaurus had a long neck, but it couldn't hold its head up very high. Its heart wasn't strong enough to pump blood that far up.

Tyrannosaurus had about 60 pointed **bone-crunching** teeth. Each tooth was about as long as a piece of printer paper is wide.

Tyrannosaurus

The **arms** of a Tyrannosaurus were only **about** 1 metre long, but they were **very strong**. Paleontologists don't know what the dinosaur used its arms for.

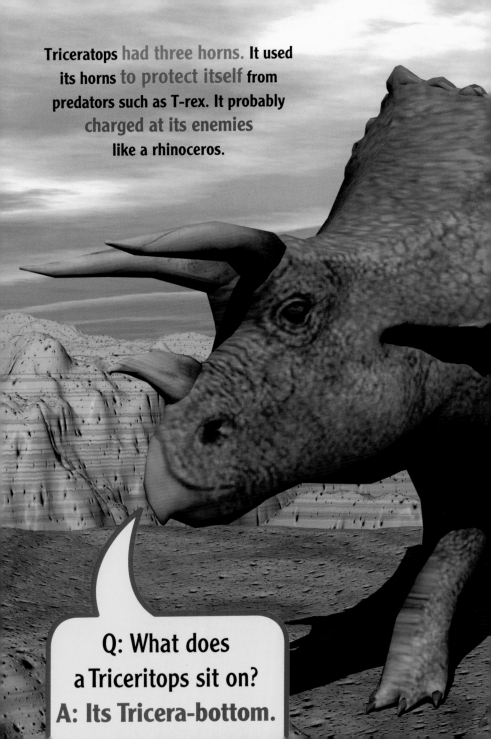

Triceratops had three horns. It used its horns to protect itself from predators such as T-rex. It probably charged at its enemies like a rhinoceros.

Q: What does a Triceritops sit on?
A: Its Tricera-bottom.

Triceratops ate only plants. It used its bird-like beak to clip off tough vegetation.

Triceratops

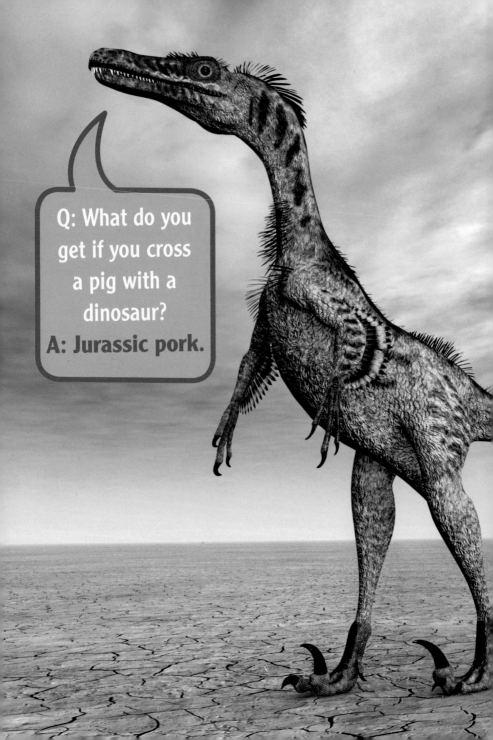

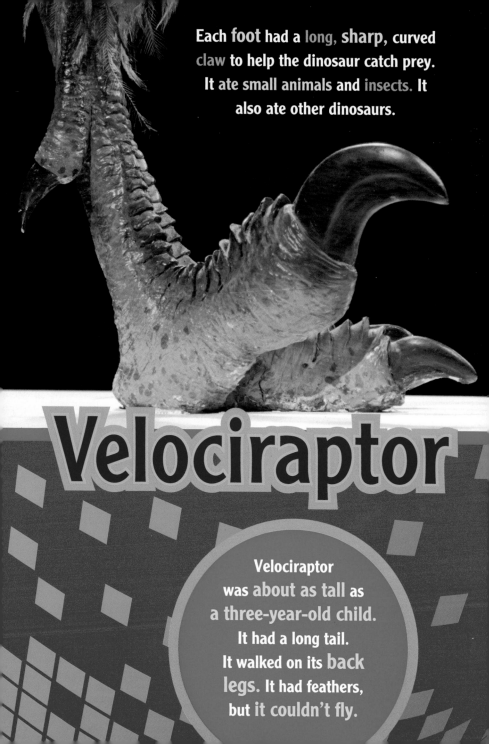

Each foot had a long, **sharp**, curved claw to help the dinosaur catch prey. It ate small animals and insects. It also ate other dinosaurs.

Velociraptor

Velociraptor was about as tall as a three-year-old child. It had a long tail. It walked on its back legs. It had feathers, but it couldn't fly.

Ankylosaurus was like **a tank.** Its whole body was **covered** with hard, bony plates and spikes. Only its **belly** didn't have armour.

It was **very big,** so it had to **eat a lot** of plants **every day.** Eating so many plants meant that Ankylosaurus **probably farted a lot.**

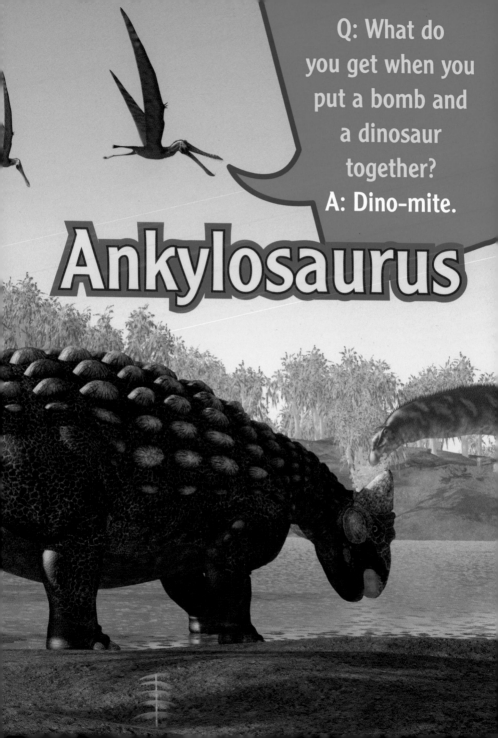

Ankylosaurus

Q: What do you get when you put a bomb and a dinosaur together? A: Dino-mite.

Diplodocus was one of the longest dinosaurs. It was as long as three school buses. Its tail was almost twice as long as its body.

It used its long tail like a whip. Paleontologists think that it used its tail to protect itself from other dinosaurs.

Pteranodon wasn't a dinosaur and it wasn't a bird. It was a **flying reptile**. It **lived** during the same **time** as dinosaurs.

Pteranodon

Q: Why can't you hear a pteranodon using the bathroom? A: Because the "p" is silent.

Pteranodon didn't have any teeth. It probably ate fish.

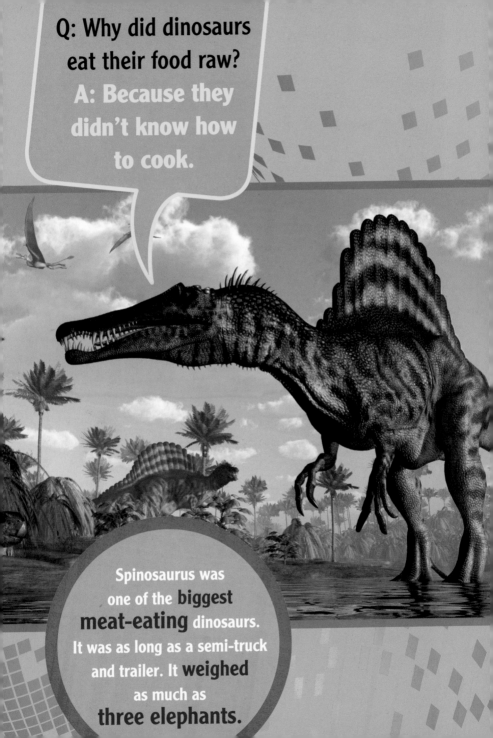

Q: Why did dinosaurs eat their food raw?
A: Because they didn't know how to cook.

Spinosaurus was one of the biggest meat-eating dinosaurs. It was as long as a semi-truck and trailer. It weighed as much as three elephants.

Spinosaurus

Compsognathus

Compsognathus had **hollow bones,** much like modern birds. It may have **had feathers.** Paleontologists think that **birds** might have **evolved** from dinosaurs like this one.

It **ate** small animals such as **lizards** and **insects.**

The **crest** on its skull was a long, curved pipe. It could make deep, loud sounds. The crest also helped Parasaurolophus **hear** better.

Parasaurolophus

Q: What do you call a dinosaur with a big vocabulary?
A: A thesaurus.

Parasaurolophus could walk on two legs or on four legs. It ate plants.

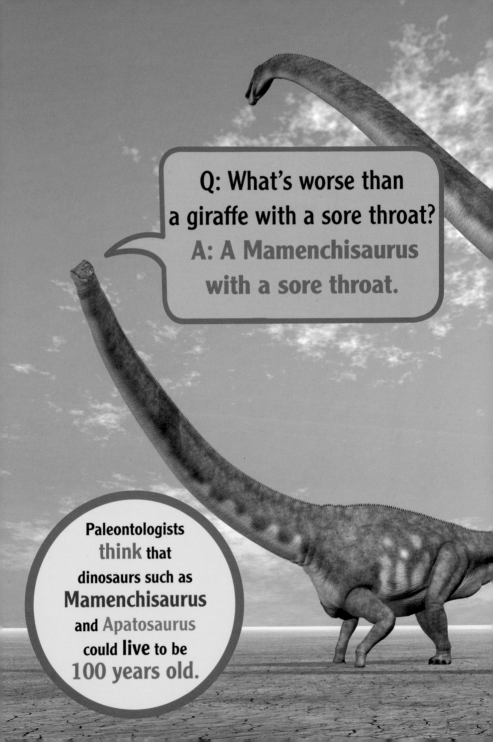

Mamenchisaurus

Mamenchisaurus had an **extremely long** neck. Its **neck** was as long as the rest of its **body** plus its **tail**.

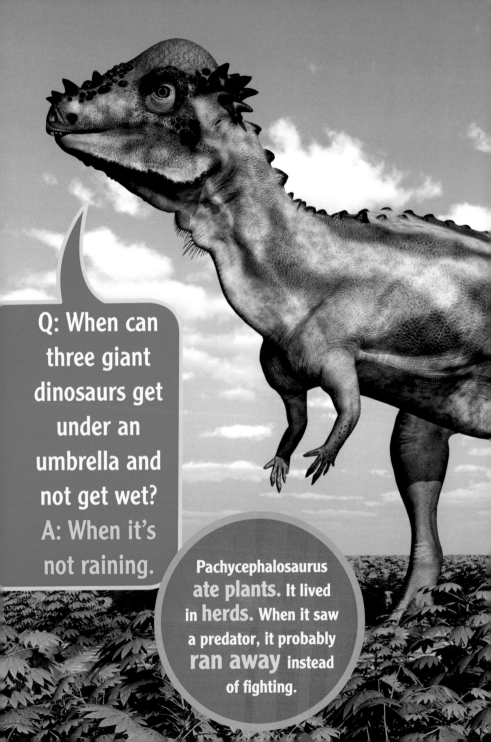

Q: When can three giant dinosaurs get under an umbrella and not get wet? A: When it's not raining.

Pachycephalosaurus ate plants. It lived in herds. When it saw a predator, it probably ran away instead of fighting.

Pachycephalosaurus

The domed skull
was up to
25 centimetres thick.
That's as thick
as dinner plate
is wide.

Brachiosaurus

Its **nostrils** were on the top of its head. They were very large. That means Brachiosaurus probably had a **good** **sense** of smell.

Ichthyosaurs were reptiles that lived in the water. They had to swim to the surface to breathe air.

Ichthyosaur

There were many kinds of Ichthyosaurs. The smallest ones were only 1 metre long. The biggest ones were about 16 metres long. That's as long as three cars.

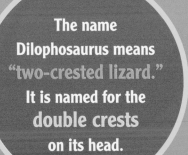

The name **Dilophosaurus** means **"two-crested lizard."** It is named for the **double crests** on its head.

Dilophosaurus was **a meat eater.** It lived in small groups. It could **run very fast.**

Dilophosaurus

Gigantoraptor

Gigantoraptor looked like a **huge** ostrich. It was twice as tall as a **human**. It had a **big beak** but no teeth.

Q: Where did Gigantoraptor buy things?
A: At a dino-store.

Gigantoraptor had feathers, but it couldn't fly. It had very strong legs and could run very fast.

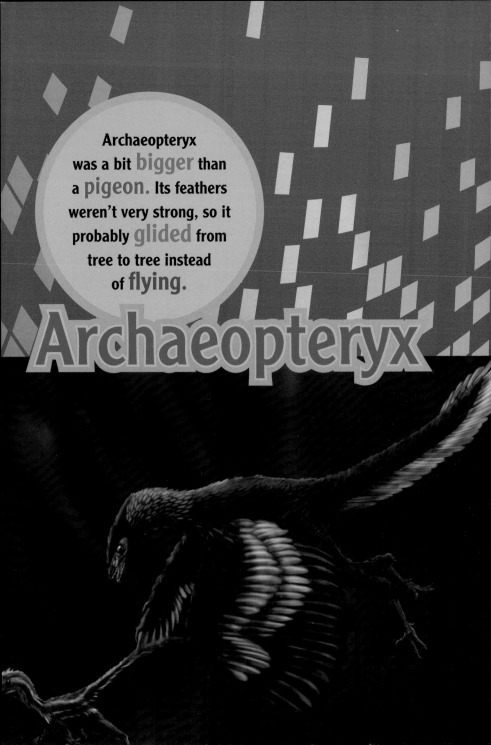

Archaeopteryx was a bit bigger than a pigeon. Its feathers weren't very strong, so it probably glided from tree to tree instead of flying.

Archaeopteryx

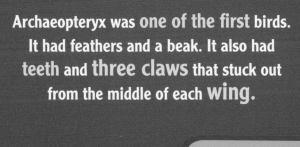

Archaeopteryx was one of the first birds. It had feathers and a beak. It also had teeth and three claws that stuck out from the middle of each wing.

Q: Why did Archaeopteryx catch the worm? A: Because it was an early bird.

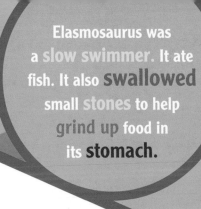

Elasmosaurus was a **slow swimmer**. It ate fish. It also **swallowed** small **stones** to help **grind up** food in its **stomach**.

Elasmosaurus

Elasmosaurus was a kind of **plesiosaur**. Plesiosaurs were reptiles that **lived in oceans**. They **breathed** air.

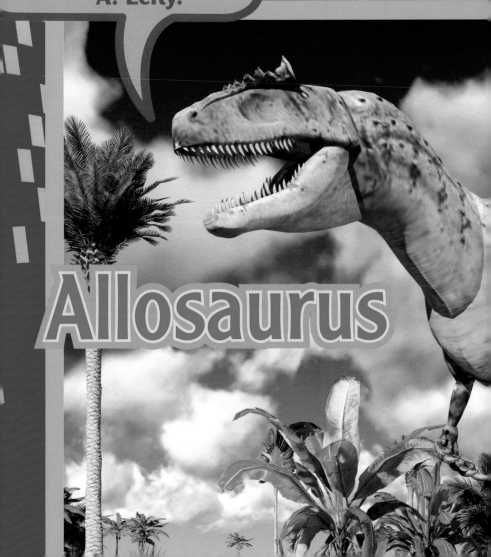

Q: What do you call someone who put their right hand in the mouth of an Allosaurus?

A: Lefty.

Allosaurus

Allosaurus was about the same size as a Tyrannosaurus. It had small horns above its eyes and ridges from the horns to its nostrils.

Its short arms had three fingers each. Each finger had a claw. The claws were 15 centimetres long. That's as long as a $5 bank note.

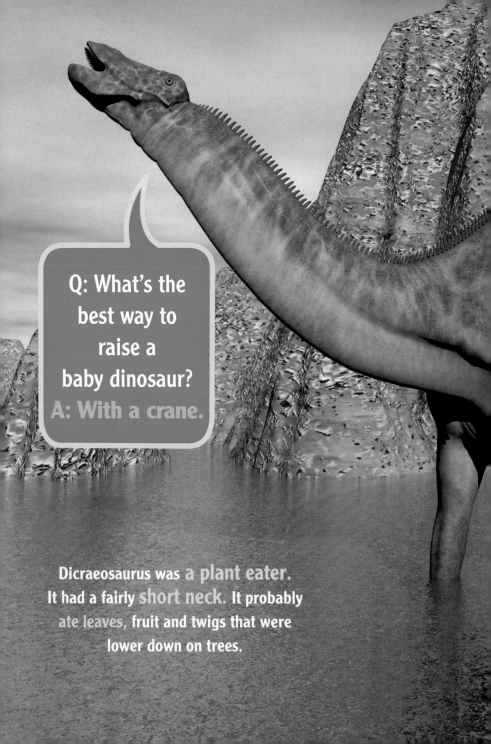

Q: What's the best way to raise a baby dinosaur?
A: With a crane.

Dicraeosaurus was a plant eater. It had a fairly short neck. It probably ate leaves, fruit and twigs that were lower down on trees.

Dicraeosaurus

It had a double row of **spines** along its back. They might have **helped** the dinosaur maintain its body temperature or they may have been for defence.

Utahraptor

Utahraptor was
the largest dinosaur
raptor. It was almost
8 metres long. It probably
had feathers.

Q: What did the dinosaur say after the accident?
A: I'm so saurus.

All raptors had large, **curved claws** on their back feet. They used the claws to **tear apart** their prey. Utahraptor's claws were almost **as long** as a **dinner plate** is wide.

Deinonychus

Deinonychus was a meat eater. It was one of the smartest dinosaurs. Its bite was about as strong as the bite of an alligator.

This dinosaur could run very fast. It hunted in packs. It used the large claws on its back feet to catch and tear apart its prey.

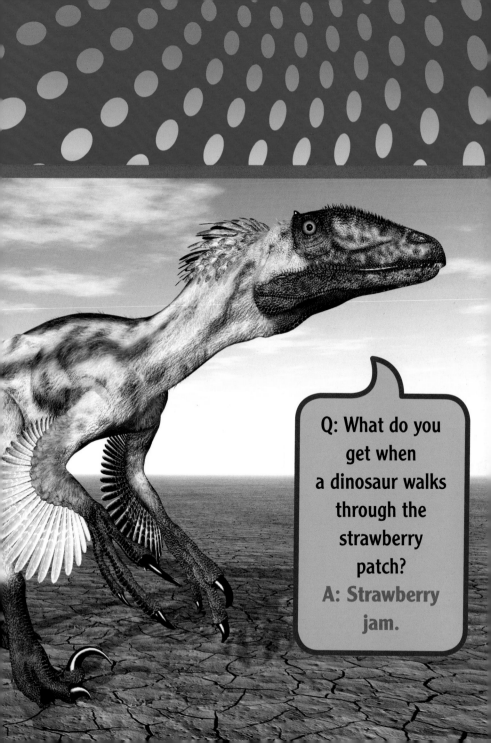

Carnotaurus

Imprints of skin in **fossils** show that Carnotaurus had scales. It also had bony **lumps** all over its body.

Q: What do you call it when a dinosaur has a car accident?
A: A Tyrannosaurus wreck.

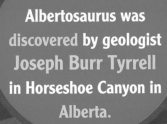

Albertosaurus was discovered by geologist Joseph Burr Tyrrell in Horseshoe Canyon in Alberta.

Albertosaurus

Albertosaurus was related to Tyrannosaurus. It was a bit smaller and lived a few million years earlier.

Q: Where does a dinosaur sit when it comes to visit?
A: Anywhere it wants to.

Tylosaurus was a large lizard that lived in seas and oceans. It was longer than a school bus. It was the largest marine predator.

Tylosaurus captured
prey with its long, pointed
teeth. It even had teeth
on the roof of its mouth.
It ate fish, sharks,
plesiosaurs and
even sea birds.

Tylosaurus

Q: How can you tell if there's a dinosaur in the refrigerator?
A: The door won't close.

Camarasaurus ate plants. It swallowed leaves and plants whole, without chewing. It also ate stones. The stones helped grind up the plants in its stomach.

Camarasaurus had **five toes** on each foot. The inside toes each had a **large, sharp claw**. The dinosaur could use the claws to **defend itself**.

Camarasaurus

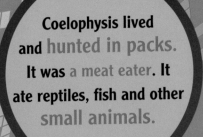

Coelophysis lived and hunted in packs. It was a meat eater. It ate reptiles, fish and other small animals.

Coelophysis

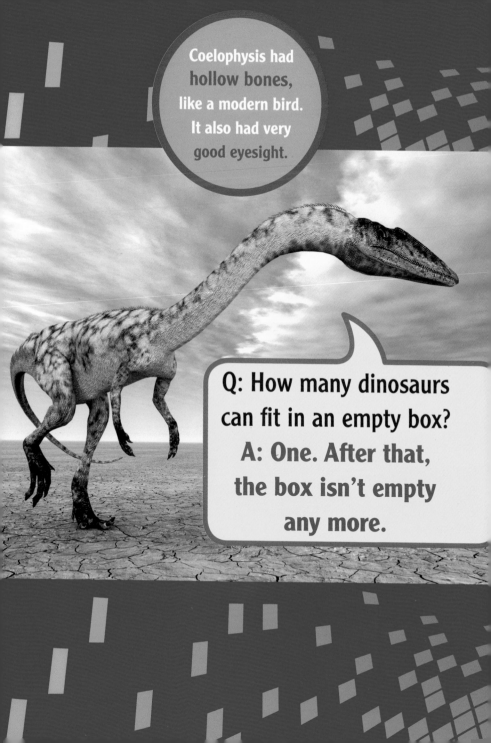

Q: What do dinosaurs have that no other animals have?
A: Baby dinosaurs.

Maiasaura was the first dinosaur whose skeleton was found with fossilized baby dinosaurs, nests and eggs. Maiasaura means "good mother lizard."

The female Maiasaura didn't sit on the nest. She covered the eggs with rotting plants to keep them warm. She sat beside the nest to protect it.

Maiasaura

The Publisher: KidsWorld Books

Library and Archives Canada Cataloguing in Publication

Dinosaur jokes / Einstein Sisters.

ISBN 978-0-9940069-7-4 (pbk.)

1. Dinosaurs—Juvenile humor. 2. Dinosaurs—Miscellanea—Juvenile literature. 3. Wit and humor, Juvenile. 4. Dinosaurs—Juvenile literature. I. Einstein Sisters, author

PS8375.D56 2015   jC818'.602   C2015-902881-7

Cover Images: Front cover: Tyrannosaurus © Ingram Publishing/Thinkstock; background © Bartfett/Thinkstock. *Back cover:* Dilophosaurus © MR1805/Thinkstock; Camarasaurus © Elenarts/Thinkstock.

Background Graphics: pixels, Misko Kordic/Thinkstock, 2, 5, 8, 9, 10, 11, 15, 18, 19, 20, 22, 23, 24, 25, 26, 27, 31, 32, 34, 35, 38, 39, 40, 41, 44, 45, 47, 48, 49, 52, 53, 56, 57, 60, 61, 62, 63; abstract background, Maryna Borsevych/Thinkstock, 37, 42, 43, 50, 51, 55; abstract swirl, hakkiarslan/Thinkstock, 13, 49.

Photo Credits: From Thinkstock: 3dalhia, 13; Andreas Meyer, 32, 38, 47, 58–59; blueringmedia, 41; CoreyFord, 2, 16–17, 18–19, 26–27, 34–35, 43, 48, 50, 60; danielfromspain, 15; Elena Duvernay, 9, 24; Elenarts, 12–13, 20–21, 39; Jozef Sedmak, 11; Jultud, 4; Lefteris, 45; leonello calvetti, 7, 10, 23, 31; Lida Xing&Yi Liu&FunkMonk, 53; Linda Bucklin, 8, 22; mariephoto28, 46–47; MR1805, 6–7, 14, 28–29, 30–31, 33, 36, 42, 50–51, 52, 56, 57, 61; Naz-3D, 15; satori13, 44–45; Steffen Foerster, 5; walbyent, 37. *From Dreamstime:* Aliencat, 25; LeoCalvett, 63; Mengzhang, 62. *From Wikipedia:* Durbed, 40; Emily Willoughby, 48–49; Karkemish, 55. *From Flickr:* Neil Conway, 54.

We acknowledge the financial support of the Government of Canada. Nous reconnaissons l'appui financier du gouvernement du Canada.

Funded by the Government of Canada
Financé par le gouvernement du Canada | Canadä

PC: 38-5